The Introvert's Guide to Entrepreneurship

How to Make the Most Out of Your Strengths and Become a Successful Entrepreneur

By Nate Nicholson

Subscribe to My Newsletter

Sign up for my entrepreneurship newsletter at http://eepurl.com/bbVcYX to receive a completely free ebook I used to sell for $2.99 – *15 Steps to Better Time Management and Higher Effectiveness*. It will teach you how to become a more effective entrepreneur who achieves more with less.

You'll also get exclusive updates about my new titles. Subscribers of my newsletter who are willing to write reviews have the opportunity to get free advance reader copies of my new books.

Don't worry – I don't send emails more often than once per week (and usually less often than that).

CONTENTS

Introduction

It appears the business world prefers and rewards extroverts and their smooth social skills. After all, so many well-known entrepreneurs are famous because of their ability to connect with other people. If it weren't for their incredible people skills, it's doubtful they would achieve even half of what they had.

Introverts, on the other hand, are frequently hidden behind the curtains. Clients don't see them. Introverted entrepreneurs usually don't get much recognition for their efforts (not that it really means anything to them) and sometimes don't even work in the company directly (they may be better suited to own the company and delegate its day-to-day operations to someone else).

As an introvert, you possess numerous strengths that extroverts lack. These skills can help you grow a successful company just as well as an extrovert would. In some cases, your unique skill set may even transform the entire company.

What type of business is good for introverts? How should you manage it (or should you manage it at all)? What should you do to avoid burnout from your entrepreneurial endeavors? What types of businesses are right for introverts? How do you validate your business idea in an introvert-friendly way? This book will answer all these questions, and many more.

By the end of this book, you'll understand how you can use your introversion as the motor of your entrepreneurial journey. It will no longer hold you back from starting or running your own business.

Are You an Introvert?

There are three types of personalities. Everybody knows two of them: introversion and extroversion. There's one more type of personality – ambiversion. It falls directly in the middle between introversion and extroversion.

Nobody is either 100% extrovert or 100% introvert. We all exhibit both introverted and extroverted behaviors. Look at the following diagram:

Few, if any people, are exactly at either end. Most of us fall somewhere between one of the three arrows between ambiversion and extroversion or introversion. Here are a couple common traits of introverts:

1. You can be described as reserved, quiet or private. You are overwhelmed by too much stimulation.

2. You prefer a slower pace and time for contemplation. Spontaneity isn't your friend.

3. You tend to think things through. There's a never-ending inner monologue in your head.

4. You would rather observe than be the center of attention. Most introverts tend to look at things from a safe distance.

5. You prefer solitude to social activities (but you don't necessarily fear social encounters).

If you agree with the above statements, you're most likely introverted.

If you haven't done so already, I urge you to test yourself using the Myers-Briggs Type Indicator test so you can better understand the key aspects of your introversion and other personal traits. There are 16 types, which are referred to by an abbreviation of four letters:

ESTJ: extroversion (E), sensing (S), thinking (T), judgment (J)

INFP: introversion (I), intuition (N), feeling (F), perception (P)

You can easily find a free test online – just type something like "Myers-Briggs Type Indicator test" in Google. Here's one of them I like the most: http://www.16personalities.com/free-personality-test. Once you complete the test, it will give you detailed information about your type. Prepare for an interesting lecture that will help you uncover your strengths and weaknesses.

Such tests won't tell you how to live your life, but they will help you better understand your decision making process, which in turn will affect your entrepreneurial skills.

Now that you know your type, let's explore the fascinating world of introversion and entrepreneurship. In the first chapter of the book, we'll discuss your strengths as an introvert and their potential effect on your business.

Chapter 1: Your 5 Main Strengths to Help You Become an Entrepreneur

While you don't possess the ability to spend hours among others, it doesn't mean you don't have any skills to help you on your entrepreneurial journey. Introversion comes with a pretty useful mix of strengths you can use to become a successful entrepreneur. You may not even be aware you have all these attributes, yet they're shared by almost all introverts.

Combine these skills with your unique strengths and you have a powerful mix of traits to start and run a successful company.

Let's dig deeper into each of your five main fortes and see how you can make the most out of them to achieve success in business.

Strategic Mind and Big Picture Thinking

Big picture thinking and the ability to go deep are two of the most important attributes of a successful entrepreneur. Introverts are introspective souls who like to spend hours pondering "what if" scenarios. And guess what? This is exactly what you need as an entrepreneur. Long-term planning is one of the keys to grow a successful company that won't fold at the first sign of problems.

Entrepreneurs who care too much about the little details forget about the 80/20 Principle – 80% of outcome is the result of 20% of effort, not the other way. In other words, the ability to focus on the most important aspects of your business will help grow it multiple times faster than dabbling into the little details.

Big picture thinking is useful, yet it can also be dangerous, because at some point the little details can add up to big things.

But here's an interesting thing – as an introvert, you can switch from big picture thinking to a more detailed approach.

Introverts don't get distracted as easily as extroverts. We don't need so much external stimulation, therefore we can spend time with things we already know and improve upon them. While extroverts are busy charging their batteries spending time with other people, introverts recharge in solitude, planning the next business moves.

A strategic mind is closely related to big picture thinking. If you have the ability to focus on the most important things, you're also capable of making long-term plans. Your strategic mind will help you set up your business the right way from the ground up instead of having to change its key aspects when it's already established.

The difference between extroverts and introverts can be described better by the story about the tortoise and the hare. The tortoise may be slow, but it isn't reckless like the hare. In the end, it's the tortoise that wins because what matters in entrepreneurship is the process, not the event.

Most newbie entrepreneurs make the mistake of thinking about a single event that will turn their entire business into a huge success. In reality, taking a company from the first customer to a national success is dull and requires repeating the same things over and over again. Extroverts who like the rush associated with new things may not persevere long enough to achieve this kind of success.

As an introvert, you have the ability to go beyond the surface and keep digging until you find the treasure. In comparison, extroverts may be a bit more restless and constantly drill new holes instead of digging just one deep enough to find the treasure chest.

You can only design a working process if you have the ability to strategize and forecast how your process will be working either a few weeks, a few months, or a few years from now.

Introverts are inwards-oriented, which makes them more prone to reflection and forecasting. Pans for the next 5 or 10 years aren't as useful in today's fast-moving world as they were in the 20th century. However, the ability to prepare for the future is still the difference between the business that fails when faced with a big problem and the business that perseveres and grows stronger.

Determination

Introverts don't like to skim the surface of things. If an introvert finds something interesting, she'll keep at it as long as she's satisfied with the end result. It's one of the most desirable attributes an entrepreneur can possess, because everything in business takes time.

As an introvert, you have the ability to look deep into yourself to find the passion that will fuel you on your entrepreneurial journey. Not all extroverts possess such a strong ability to look deeply into themselves to discover a powerful reason why they should keep going. Their motivation may be more dependent on other people, and any kind of external motivation is always weaker than the motivation that comes from within you.

If you don't have the ability to come up with a powerful mission for your business, it's going to be extremely hard to grow a lasting business. After all, why keep toiling away if you don't really know why you are doing it?

Persistence is a powerful advantage in today's competitive business world when so many entrepreneurs fail because when faced with a problem, they'd rather give up than solve it. Use your inquisitive, introverted mind to keep going and find solutions where others drop out in pursue of something easier (and before they realize nothing is easier, you'll be well on your way toward success in business).

Jack-of-All-Trades

Most introverts spend so much time alone they pass countless hours learning about new things by reading books, articles, and blogs. It's their way of recharging the batteries. In the meantime, extroverts spend their time with other people, getting their high from meeting new people and receiving the attention of others.

Your vast knowledge is of tremendous value when you want to start or grow a business. New brain cell connections, the result of your learning, make it easier to see similarities among seemingly unrelated phenomena. They will also help you make better decisions.

Being a jack-of-all-trades will help you be a flexible entrepreneur – an entrepreneur who can easily pivot if he sees that the current path will not lead him where he wants to go. Persistence is a skill to admire, but it takes even more prowess to know when to give up and try something else.

While it's definitely useful to be a specialist in your chosen field, as an entrepreneur you should have at least some basic knowledge about many different things – marketing, product development, customer service, management, and copywriting, just to name a few. All of these skills will help you either get your business off the ground by yourself or delegate the key aspects to the right people.

The best entrepreneurs are people who constantly learn new things and apply them in their businesses to gain a competitive edge by constant innovation. It turns out that all the hours you spent alone reading various things were actually pretty productive for you.

Please bear in mind that your appetite for knowledge may also be a weakness. When finishing one business book, don't be tempted to just read another and another book. Instead, spend your time implementing the advice from the first book.

Some entrepreneurs (especially beginners) fall into the trap of reading more than they work. As a result, they have a lot of theoretical knowledge, but they have no idea how to apply it in the real world to their business.

I've been such a person for a long time. My workday consisted of reading book after book. It gave me the fake sense of accomplishment in the same way self-help literature can give you a boost of self-esteem. After all, you're doing something if you're reading a book, right?

Wrong.

Reading business or self-help books has its place in your schedule, but it should never take away the time you spend implementing the advice. Always have your end-goal in mind when reading new business books. Don't just read them for enjoyment – treat each book as an investment in your business. You're not going to get a return if you put the book away without applying any of its tips to your company.

Looking from a Distance

Introverts have a need to escape from the world and recharge in solitude. Their habit of spending so much time alone can actually be extremely beneficial for their company.

By spending time away from the hustle and bustle of your business, you can gain a fresh perspective on current challenges. Entrepreneurs who never take the time to get away from the company may become too involved in it. Consequently, the obvious solutions to their problems may be out of their sight.

When you start a business, make sure to keep spending ample time alone. Time spent in solitude will help you recharge your batteries and look at your company from a distance. Only then can you see the forest for the trees and notice things that may not have been obvious in the midst of managing your business processes.

Don't forget that people make the best decisions when they're fully rested. You rest when you spend time alone, so don't consider it your weakness when running a business – it's your way of recharging to help you make good decisions.

Hard work is often overrated. Many entrepreneurs think that the more hours they put in, the better their results will be. As a result, they increase the risk of missing potential problems in the company. Their constant meddling may also make things worse.

Your time alone is a treasure – both for your mental health and for your company. Use it to recharge your batteries and refresh your brain.

The Ability to Listen

Introverts don't like to draw unnecessary attention to them. While extroverts thrive when other people pay attention to them, introverts would rather stay in the back of the room and watch things from a safe distance. As a result, they usually have pretty developed listening skills and don't interrupt other people when they're speaking.

The ability to listen is one of the most powerful skills in life. In business, the ability to listen can help you notice problems that would have otherwise gone unnoticed before it's too late to do something about them.

The ability to listen attentively will help you in negotiations, when managing your employees, when dealing with your clients and collecting feedback to improve your services or products.

When an extrovert would interrupt another person, you would listen carefully and potentially learn something that could transform your company.

By putting the spotlight on other people, you can look at your company from another point of view – the one that you would have never had with only your own insights.

If you want to learn more about how to listen actively, read *Nonviolent Communication*: *A Language of Life* by Marshall B. Rosenberg. It depicts a simple introvert-friendly process to connect with people on a deeper level. You can apply it to both personal relationships as well as the professional ones.

Chapter 2: Your 5 Most Harmful Weaknesses that Can Affect Your Business

Some aspects of introversion are extremely useful when running a business, but just like with everything else, there are two sides to the coin.

Your introversion can lead to numerous problems in your company if you aren't aware of your limitations or the behaviors you find normal that other people recognize as strange or unfriendly.

In the following chapter, we'll explore some of the most common weaknesses of introverts. We'll talk about how and when they can affect your business and what to do to reduce their negative influence on your ventures.

Over-thinking

Since introverts are so inwards-oriented, they tend to overthink things. Analysis paralysis, the result of over-thinking, leads to passivity. It can be harmful when you linger on for too long and don't make a decision at the right moment. Taking too much time to make decisions can be disastrous in today's fast-moving world.

The best way to deal with this weakness is to pay close attention to your decision making process. If you're taking too long to make a decision, set short deadlines to avoid paralyzing your whole company.

Keep in mind that according to Parkinson's Law, work expands so as to fill the time available for its completion. If you give yourself plenty of time to make a decision, you'll probably make it just before the deadline, not sooner. If you set a short, improbable deadline, you'll surprise yourself by reaching your goal on time, much sooner that you thought was capable.

Over-thinking can also lead to waiting too long to start a business. Some introverts want to know everything before they do something, which is never a given in business. If you try looking for a perfect answer to each potential problem, you'll never start.

Don't become a wantrepreneur, a person who wants to become an entrepreneur, but never does because she's paralyzed with too many choices and doesn't know which one is perfect (hint: no choice is ideal).

So many people don't start any business because they want to wait until they come up with a perfect idea. Introverts would also add to this list of excuses uncertainty and hundreds of "what if" scenarios. If you want to become an entrepreneur, take action. It's the most important quality that discerns entrepreneurs at heart from people who just wish their lives would be different.

Being Judgmental

Some introverts feel so misunderstood by other people that they grow bitter of them. Moreover, they may feel superior to extroverts because they can't accept the differences in their personalities.

The world, and especially the Western world, rewards extroverted behaviors in business, but it doesn't mean there's no place for introverts. A well-oiled company should derive its power from both extroverted and introverted qualities.

Be personality-agnostic. As long as someone gets the job done in an effective manner, his personality shouldn't matter at all. Avoid judging people by their personality. Both extroverts and introverts can bring a lot to the table – if you only let them.

If you have never understood the behavior or needs of an extrovert, perhaps it's time to learn about them before you hire one. Just like some extroverts don't understand introverts because they have never thought of learning about their needs, so won't you understand an extrovert before you understand what drives her in life.

Don't be afraid to break out of your shell from time to time and try doing things reserved for extroverts. It's a good exercise in stepping outside your comfort zone and learning about a different way of handling things. When you make an effort to understand a different outlook on life, you'll find yourself less judgmental.

Dislike of Collaboration

Large groups of people can be so distracting to introverts that they'll start seeking escape rather than contributing to the group. And why blame them – their strength comes from their individualism, not from conformity.

Introverts don't work well in large groups of people, and they usually dislike most forms of collaboration. They'd rather work on their own so they don't have to make compromises and spend too much time with others.

While this weakness will not affect you much when you're a solopreneur, it can harm you a lot when you're trying to build a company that relies on more people to provide the services or products.

The solution is to appoint someone to take care of managing the groups. If you dislike collaboration, you'll exhibit it around other people. Outsource your weaknesses and focus on what you do best.

If you have never gotten along with other people when collaborating, consider a business that relies only on you and your skills. For some introverts, being forced to depend on other people or collaborate with them may be an extremely draining and frustrating experience.

Even with the most genius business idea and perfect execution, a business can fail if the owner hates the day-to-day of his company (unless he's not directly involved in it).

Dislike of Networking

As entrepreneur Porter Gale says, your network is your net worth. Networking can help you grow your company much faster than if you were running it as if you were operating in a vacuum. However, most introverts hate networking, and find it hard to make small talk with strangers.How do you deal with this weakness? Change the way you network. Networking doesn't have to be about attending conferences or large events and speaking with as many people as possible.

You can grow a smaller alliance with like-minded people and spend your time deepening your relationships with them. In fact, a mastermind of several people can help you grow much faster than approaching networking as if it were a contest of who has more acquaintances.

Thanks to the Internet, you don't even have to leave your home (or office). Email, which is probably your preferred form of communication, is a perfect way to reach out to people in your industry and network with them. In fact, it's more time-efficient than attending dozens of events in hopes of meeting someone interesting.

When establishing contact with other people, always think in terms of what they can gain from working with you, not the other way around. When you approach everyone from the position of helping them, you'll increase your chances of establishing a close business relationship.

Nobody likes receiving random inquiries from strangers. Most people won't reply to them, and the ones who do may click "reply" only to tell you to never email them again.

Don't make the rookie mistake of thinking your business is the most important thing in the world. Use your ability to be introspective to find out what the other side can benefit from networking with you and use it to develop the relationship.

As an introvert, you're much better at strengthening relationships than making new contacts. Turn your weakness into a strength by nurturing relationships with just a few chosen people. It pays to focus on the best people in the industry. Don't forget about the key to making new contacts – the art of the follow-up. Don't just tell people you have to catch up. Do it. A quick email won't cost you anything, but it can create miracles when building strong business relationships.

One of the lesser-known qualities of introverts is their preference of honesty. Research[i] shows that the more reflective a person is, the more honest she becomes. Since introverts are more reflective than extroverts[ii], they are more likely to be honest.

Being an honest person means you can't stand phony networking – pleasantries exchanged for a mere purpose of extracting something from another person. While it can negatively affect the first impression you'll make on a potential business contact, it can also help you with straight-shooter types.

Being Reserved

Most introverts don't act comfortable around strangers. If you're an entrepreneur, unless you create a company that's mostly automated or delegate the day-to-day tasks to someone else, you'll have to deal with strangers on a daily basis – new employees, clients, and suppliers.

By learning the basics of how to make small talk and interact with strangers, you'll become much more effective at working with other people. Moreover, you'll reduce the risk of potential clients feeling uncomfortable around you. What you may consider a waste of time (purposeless small talk or the so-called "wining and dining" of a client) is for some people a necessary step before establishing a business relationship.

The hardest part of starting a company for an introvert may be getting the initial customers. As the founder of the company, it should be you who's interacting with the first clients. You do it to gain personal feedback and understand your market better. Your employees can do this job for you, but it will turn to your detriment when you don't understand how the mind of your client works.

How do you deal with this weakness? I'm afraid the only solution is to spend a lot of time alone to recharge your batteries and then grit your teeth and meet with your clients. First-hand knowledge is the best kind of feedback you can ever get when starting your venture.

If your business grows well, you can always hire someone to take care of all customer relationships for you. After all, as an introvert, you'll probably be much more effective when doing a job that isn't about human interaction.

Chapter 3: How to Lead Your Company as an Introvert

One of the first words that comes to mind when thinking about entrepreneurship is the word "leadership." No company can grow quickly and become successful without a leader. In this chapter, we'll explore the aspect of leadership for introverts and discuss how you can lead your company in an introvert-friendly way (if you decide to lead it).

How do you lead people if you're an introvert who would much rather spend time by himself than by telling other people what to do? Should you act as an extrovert or try to skip the responsibilities of a leader altogether?

There are two approaches. You can either use the non-authoritarian style of leadership that relies on listening to other people and giving them freedom to make their own decisions or delegate your responsibilities as a leader.

3 Key Strategies to Lead Your Company as an Introvert

If you think of leadership, you may think of people who are constantly around others, who tell them what exactly to do, how to do it and when to do it. In reality, leadership is about guiding other people. Whether you do it the gentle way or the aggressive way depends on your personality.

As an introvert, you'll probably prefer the gentle way of leadership. This style of leading will make the most out of your strengths while reducing the effect of your weaknesses. Below are the three key strategies that will help you lead your company as an introvert.

1. Listen to your employees

One of your strengths as an introvert is the ability to listen attentively. Use it when leading your employees. Reward initiative and listen to their feedback. Make your employees the stars of your business by putting the spotlight on them.

Many employees need praise more than they need a raise. And while it's easier to "bribe" someone, kind words in many instances work just as well or even better – and they're free.

Give your employees freedom, but make sure you trust them so you won't question their every decision. Back them up and your company will grow. Criticize them and your company will be divided.

One of the most well-known entrepreneurs who uses this kind of approach is British billionaire Richard Branson. In all his Virgin companies, employees are encouraged to speak their minds and take the initiative to run their own projects. Consequently, all new employees know they can always suggest a new way of doing things. They also know they'll be encouraged to try their idea, and perhaps get a promotion if it turns out to have potential to transform the company.

Make it your company's policy to encourage feedback from your employees and most importantly, act on it. If your employees notice you not only listen to their feedback, but also respect it and implement it, they'll be much more eager to share their views with you.

2. Schedule one-on-one meetings

As an introvert, you'll probably have a hard time talking to a large group of people, and constantly changing your attention from one person to another.

Introverts thrive in social situations where they can focus on just one person. If you have more than just a few employees, break them into smaller groups. Ideally, schedule one-on-one meetings with each of your employees instead of a meeting with all of them.

Another benefit of this approach is that if you employ any introverts, they'll appreciate personal one-on-one feedback.

If you have more employees, consider giving some of your employees the status of a "mini-CEO," a person who makes decisions for her team while consulting with you only about more important matters.

3. Outsource and automate

The less people you have to guide, the more effectively you can lead. Introverts lead better when they can focus on each employee individually instead of working with the whole group.

Use outsourcing and automation to reduce your dependency on employees. What aspects of your business could you delegate to another company and reduce your staff? What parts of your business processes could be automated so you wouldn't need an employee to oversee them?

The best approach is to think about outsourcing and automation before hiring someone new. Automation and outsourcing are usually much cheaper than hiring an employee (as they say, overhead walks on two legs), so it makes economic sense and will help you lead better at the same time.

In an ideal world, an introvert-friendly business is a business with zero employees. If it's possible to turn your company into a virtual company with no full-time employees, do it – the freedom of not having to manage anyone is bliss for an introvert.

Thanks to the Internet, you too can run a profitable business without any employees or with remote workers whom you don't need to see on a daily basis. Some extremely successful online companies are run by a remote team working from all over the world. Introvert-friendly email is their primary form of contact.

One example of such a company is The Truth about Six-Pack Abs, a digital company created and managed by Mike Geary. He has a small team that helps him with customer service and site maintenance. Even though he has no real office and doesn't see his employees on a regular basis, his company generates almost $1 million in revenue per month.

Should You Lead at All?

Not all introverts are suited to be leaders. If you prefer to spend much more time alone than with people, then managing your employees on a day-to-day basis may be extremely draining for you.

Consequently, it may be a wise idea to delegate leadership to someone else. It sounds strange to delegate leadership, but it's a strategy that's been followed by quite a lot of entrepreneurs.

One of the most notable examples is Richard Branson, who said, "Entrepreneurs have the dynamism to get something started . . . Yet an entrepreneur is not necessarily good at the nuts and bolts of running a business.[iii]" In other words, Richard believes that entrepreneurs are good at starting businesses, but they may not necessarily be good managers or leaders.

Richard Branson practices what he preaches. As he wrote in his book *Screw Business as Usual*, "I believe firmly in delegation and good people were running each of Virgin's three hundred companies worldwide. These managers were so competent that on average it often took me just a few minutes each week on the phone, checking in with them.[iv]"

Please keep in mind that the classic definition of entrepreneurship is to shift economic resources out of an area of lower and into an area of higher productivity and greater yield. If your ability to lead can hinder your company's growth, it's your job to find someone who's a better leader.

After all, it's only when you can remove yourself from the equation and have your business continue to run and grow that you have a well-oiled machine.

Chapter 4: Introversion, Entrepreneurship, and Other People

Introverts don't relish social interaction like extroverts do. They recharge their batteries when spending time alone. How can an introverted entrepreneur grow his company and balance it with his need to spend time alone?

The most effective way to deal with this problem is to choose the right type of business that won't require so much social interaction. But what if you're already running a business or plan to run a business that will depend on your ability to connect with people? The answer might be to partner up with an extrovert.

Why You Should Consider an Extroverted Business Partner

One of the most notable examples of an introvert-extrovert business partnership was Steve Jobs (extrovert) and Steve Wozniak (introvert), the pair that made Apple one of the most well-known companies in the world.

Their personality traits complemented each other and helped them grow their business by focusing on what they do best. Steve Jobs became the public face of the company, while Steve Wozniak could dedicate himself to engineering – a perfect job for an introvert.

By partnering up with an extrovert, you'll take care of two things that can become troublesome once your company grows – leadership and having the public face of the company.

Nowadays, companies with visible CEOs are much more trusted than faceless corporations. As an introvert, you definitely won't enjoy the idea of being in the spotlight. By having an extroverted partner, you can let him shine while you work behind the scenes to ensure that your company provides the best products or services.

You'll have to swallow your pride when people start associating your company only with the name of your business partner, but it's for the best if it helps you maximize on your strengths.

An extroverted business partner can take care of customer relationships, marketing, employee management, and any other functions that require a lot of human interaction. He'll thrive when working with other people, while you would be completely drained of energy before the day is over.

By partnering up with an extrovert, you'll be able to focus on what you do best – tasks that require deep thinking which can be done without the constant presence of other people.

Why You Should NOT Consider an Extroverted Business Partner

Partnership with an extrovert isn't always a good idea. In fact, many people aren't suited to be good business partners. Partnerships can do a lot of harm if you're working with the wrong person.

If you aren't good at making compromises and want to do everything your way, a partnership is probably not for you. Instead of looking for a partner, look for extroverted employees who exhibit strengths in the areas in which you're weak.

I've worked with a couple partners and although none of these partnerships led to a complete disaster, they didn't work well, either. I found myself drifting away from the business because it wasn't entirely mine. My personality is too dominating to make partnerships work. If you can't stand the thought of asking your partner for permission every time you want to make a decision, go solo.

Many newbie entrepreneurs are tempted to start a business with their friend. It's one of the worst mistakes you can make – both to your business and to your friendship. Contrary to what some people believe, it's impossible to separate business life from personal life. If you care about your friend, don't partner up with her.

5 Key Attributes of a Good Business Partner for an Introvert

It's difficult to find a good business partner. Many partnerships fail because the partners can't communicate with each other or because they have a different idea about the direction of the company.

For you, as an introvert looking for an extroverted business partner, another challenge is to find someone who will be able to communicate with you given your personality. Below are the five key attributes of an extroverted business partner who will be a good fit for an introvert.

1. Great marketing skills

You market to people; therefore an extroverted entrepreneur who enjoys social interactions will find marketing easier than an introvert. The more time you spend with your clients, the more you know about how to market them. It's tricky for introverts to spend adequate time with clients, suppliers, employees and then still have energy to spend time with friends.

As an introvert, the mere thought of cold calling someone can make your hair stand on end. For an extrovert, it will be an opportunity to have a conversation. An introvert may think of a meeting with a client as a chore, while an extrovert will be looking forward to it.

These differences can make or break a company. If you want to start a business that will have to rely on personal interaction (meaning it's not a digital business where transactions are conducted through email or are automated), ask yourself if you can stomach the idea of spending so much time with other people.

As an entrepreneur, you should still understand the fundamentals of marketing even if you're an introvert. However, partnering up with an extrovert will ensure that a person who genuinely likes spending a lot of time with other people will be responsible for making the first impression.

Every marketing technique that requires you to bug other people will quickly drain you of energy. An ideal extroverted business partner should have no fear of reaching out to clients. This skill is extremely important if you're running a business that has to rely on outbound marketing – going after your client instead of waiting for him to come to you.

If you can grow your business with non-personal marketing techniques (paid traffic, email marketing, etc.), an extroverted partner for marketing purposes isn't necessary.

2. Great connections

Extroverts are good at networking, while introverts prefer a few close friends and associates to a large social network of people they don't know well.

An extroverted business partner who has a lot of connections can use the power of his network to get your company to the next level. Connections can be the most important asset an extrovert brings to a company – more important than money or know-how.

When considering a potential business partner, think about resources of a social nature – his colleagues, suppliers, his past client base, etc. Just one right partnership can dramatically enhance the sales of your company by reaching a new customer base or developing new products.

3. Non-judgmental and patient

Introverts aren't quick to make a decision – they're the tortoise, after all.

If you partner up with an extrovert who's rash and wants to make quick decisions, it will lead to numerous disagreements – unless you let him make minor decisions without asking you for permission.

Non-judgmental and patient extroverts will respect the introvert's need to take some time to make the right decision. Moreover, they will understand they can't just force you to interact with customers for 8 hours with no break and expect you to feel great afterwards.

When partnering up with an extrovert, make sure he understands the key aspects of introversion, so that he'll know what to expect from you, and why you're doings things the way you do them.

4. Focused

Since a lot of extroverts like to skim the surface of things and move on to the next shiny object, it's important to find a partner who will understand that focus is the key.

The ability to focus is much more natural to introverts than extroverts. While an introvert would relish the thought of spending a few days left completely alone, an extrovert with little to no external stimulation would go crazy.

Make sure your partner is focused enough to keep doing the same thing that's working for as long as it produces results. If you partner up with an extrovert who doesn't understand that running a company is all about developing repeatable processes in a focused way, you'll have a hard time agreeing about the key business decisions.

5. Open-minded and ready to make compromises

Introverts don't like to speak up, but they like to do things their own way. In an ideal scenario, you should partner up with an extrovert who will hold the minority stake in your company so that you can have the final say.

If you want to split the company 50/50 (not recommended, you should always own the majority), you better find an extrovert who's open-minded and ready to make compromises. If you're both stubborn and not able to find a common ground, your partnership will crumble pretty soon.

Prevent a lot of headaches and avoid 50/50 partnerships. No partnership is ever 50/50, anyway, and there should always be someone who has the final say (ideally it should be you).

Chapter 5: The Introvert's Guide to Self-Promotion

If you want to run a small business or become a solopreneur (an entrepreneur working at his home office with no employees), you'll have to learn how to promote yourself.

As an introvert, self-promotion will be difficult for you because you don't enjoy being at the center of attention. Moreover, self-promotion probably reminds you of a person that goes through the window if she can't go through the door. Few introverts are so cocksure. Most of them would rather go home than keep bugging other people.

Fortunately, as an introvert you possess some strengths that can help you replace the traditional self-promoting techniques, which require extroverted traits, with something more introvert-friendly (and equally, if not more, effective).

Your Number One Skill to Use for Your Every Self-Promotional Need

Many introverts possess great writing skills – the result of spending so much time alone with books and self-introspection, frequently in the form of writing a journal, stories, or poems.

Fortunately, one of the most effective ways to promote yourself, inbound marketing, requires great writing skills.

In essence, inbound marketing is about getting your customers to come to you instead of you chasing them. It's much more effective than old-school outbound marketing where a salesman keeps chasing after a customer until she relents.

You can draw clients to yourself in a wide variety of ways. The most common way is usually writing a blog, books, or producing any other type of written content. If you're into audio, podcasts are also an effective way to promote yourself.

Blogging is such a powerful marketing tool that for many online entrepreneurs it's the only activity they do marketing-wise. You can also benefit from blogging. As an introvert it will suit you much better than having to develop relationships in the offline word.

An additional benefit of blogging is that it makes it easy to make online friends with whom you'll be able to develop deep bonds without having to leave your home.

Writing books is another introvert-friendly activity that can help you grow your business or establish yourself as an expert in a certain niche.

Thanks to the Internet, it's pretty easy to release your own ebook and even print some physical copies of your book to hand out to potential customers. Being a published author, even if all the books were self-published, is major social proof.

Last but not least, your writing skills will be of use when reaching out to other people by email. Email is a succinct form of communication, which is a much better choice for introverts than draining phone calls. Don't be afraid to connect by email with people in your industry – some connections made this way can lead to joint ventures and other profitable partnerships.

Become a Go-To Person

If you think of networking and self-promotion, you probably think of attending conferences and events to make personal connections with fellow attendees. This way of self-promotion doesn't work well for introverts because they aren't good at approaching new people and making small talk with them.

The good news is that you don't have to approach conferences, seminars, and other events this way. Let other people come to you instead of you chasing after them – just like with inbound marketing.

Instead of listening to someone speak, become a public speaker yourself. 15 minutes or so spent talking in front of a crowd about something you're knowledgeable about may sound gruesome. However, the benefits are well worth it – people will introduce themselves to you and you won't have to approach anyone to make connections.

Moreover, public speaking isn't really as draining as you think. Introverts have the ability to go deep and talk with passion about things that interest them. Public speaking allows you to share your knowledge without anyone interrupting you. You'll probably find it less exhausting to focus on the whole room than the social interactions afterwards.

Another way to make connections without having to approach other people is to host events by yourself. By being the host instead of the guest, you become the go-to person. People will introduce themselves to you to get to know the person who organized the event. You'll feel like a VIP with little work (once you take care of logistics, of course).

If you start hosting regular events in your industry, everyone will start associating your name with the topic of the events, thus making you the expert. For introverts, it's a much better approach than attending various events and forcing yourself to approach strangers.

In the end, self-promotion is all about establishing your status as an expert. When you feel sick, you go to a doctor and listen to his advice. A doctor won't call you to ask you if you perhaps want a check-up. Become the doctor of your industry, let other people come to you, and reap the benefits.

The Key to Effective Self-Promotion

Effective self-promotion has little to do with promoting yourself. In fact, the self-serving kind of promotion should be the last thing on your list. What works best to establish yourself as an expert and get people to come to you is putting your focus on giving.

Giving, as in creating value, is the secret of all most successful solopreneurs (and entrepreneurs in general, too). The more you give, the more people you will reach. While many of them will settle for the information you shared for free, there will always be a small percentage of people who will want to know more. These people will be willing to pay you to get to know your best secrets – even if you already shared most of them for free.

All well-known bloggers are a good example of how giving can make you an authority. The first example that comes to my mind is Pat Flynn, an online entrepreneur who runs an extremely popular blog called Smart Passive Income. His main focus is on helping his audience and being as transparent as possible (to the point that he's sharing how much money he earns every month).

By putting his focus on giving more and more (instead of promoting his paid products everywhere he can) he draws more readers to his blog. Some of these readers turn into subscribers, some of them buy the products he recommends (which generates a commission for him) and some of them buy his own products. It's a win-win for all people involved.

If you also want to go this route, remember that this business is all about giving. The more you give (without expecting to get anything back), the more you receive.

Fortunately, your introverted nature will help you avoid the wrong self-serving kind of self-promotion and focus on creating more value. If you keep sharing your knowledge freely online, more and more people will come to you to get more – and reward you richly for doing so.

Chapter 6: Introvert-Friendly Businesses

In this chapter, I'll share with you the five key aspects of an introvert-friendly business. Then we'll cover some of the most common business models that play well off your strengths as an introvert.

5 Attributes of Introvert-Friendly Businesses

While you're free to run any kind of business you want, there are certain types of businesses that are more suitable for introverts. If you choose a business that requires more extroverted traits, you may quickly grow tired of it, thus forcing you to close it. Here are five attributes of introvert-friendly businesses.

Easy to Automate or Outsource

As an introvert, you much prefer spending time alone to spending time with other people. If your business requires a lot of employees to run smoothly, you may quickly become tired of constant social interaction. In fact, even if it makes a lot of money and works like clockwork, the day-to-day of such a business can kill your motivation and lead to its demise.

Can your business become fully automated? If you can't fully automate it, how passive can it become and how many employees would you need? How often would you need to talk with them? Would you constantly have to be at the location to tell them what to do?

What about outsourcing? Can you outsource various parts of your business so you can get the finished product or service from another company without having to make it yourself?

Ask yourself all of these questions before you launch a business. The best time to think about how your business is going to make you feel is before you start it. If I knew this sooner, I would avoid starting a couple companies that would never work well with my introverted personality.

In the ideal world, it should be possible to automate your business to the maximum – thanks to various tools, not people. The less people you have to depend on, the better your business will fit your introverted personality.

With Minimal Customer Interaction

When thinking about customer interaction, consider if your business can rely on email only. Businesses that require dozens of phone calls per day are a horrible choice for introverts.

Numerous phone calls will suck your energy and may cause you to seek escape from your business – frequently at the expense of your clients, who are left hanging because you just can't bear yet another social interaction.

Don't forget that a business can't be easily automated if it requires face-to-face customer interaction and/or frequent phone calls, especially if it requires your attention as the CEO because of the big deals you're making with key clients.

Introverts thrive when they can work alone. If you're forced to constantly interact with other people, it will reduce your effectiveness. Think about it before starting a business that's all about frequent face-to-face meetings with clients.

For this reason, product-based businesses (especially digital ones) are more introvert-friendly than service-based businesses.

With No Fixed Business Hours

...so you can do things at your own schedule.

Introverts like working alone with no distractions. If your business doesn't have fixed business hours (say, you're selling digital courses), you're free to work whenever you want – early in the morning or late at night.

If you have to be at your store or office at 9 PM to open and close it at 5 PM, there's not much freedom to work whenever you want. Fixed business hours will make you feel like a prisoner of your business.

For introverts, online businesses such as e-commerce stores are a much better choice than offline businesses with a physical location. Brick and mortar businesses usually don't offer the freedom to work during your most effective hours.

The only exception is when you hire enough employees to take care of all the key aspects of the business so you don't have to be physically available all the time.

Location-Independent

Introverts like to spend a lot of time alone without any other people in sight. A business that can be ran from every location in the world is a perfect choice for introverts, as it usually means you don't have to meet with your clients face-to-face and can frequently rely on emails only.

Again, online business is the right choice for you as it usually allows to have no office and can be ran from anywhere in the world where there's Internet connection.

As a general rule, if you can do without an office, don't have one. Most commercial spaces require you to sign a lease for at least a couple months, which can become a huge financial burden – especially on a startup.

Analytical

As an introvert, one of your strengths lies in analysis. Many introverts can spend hours running numbers, analyzing data and trying to notice trends to help them grow their companies faster.

Learn the basics of direct-response marketing to understand how to track your marketing investments and make sure they always bring a positive return.

Your strategic mind coupled with a business that can be easily analyzed will result in a business that grows month after month.

Types of businesses that can be easily analyzed are businesses focused on selling products. The more standardized your products are, the easier it is to collect data and draw useful conclusions from it.

Run frequent tests and dig deep into the data to grow your business the mathematical way. If it can't be measured, it can't be managed.

9 Introvert-Friendly Business Models to Consider

In this subchapter we'll discuss some of the best business models for introverts. All of these ideas fit the majority or all of the requirements listed in the previous subchapter. To make this book more evergreen, I'm not sharing any specific examples because companies constantly change. A quick Google search will help you find more than enough about each of these ideas.

SaaS

SaaS, or Software as a Service, is a great choice for introverted geeks. If you're capable of coding an application that will solve a specific problem, consider starting a SaaS company. Business-to-business SaaS companies can charge higher prices, but they usually require the CEO to interact with clients much more than in the case of business-to-consumer companies.

Most SaaS companies charge monthly or yearly, which makes it a perfect source of predictable revenue – once you generate a stable base of customers, that is.

The biggest advantage of SaaS companies for introverts is that it's easy to automate many parts of this business. However, customer service becomes an issue when your company grows to such a level that it can no longer be done by yourself or just a single employee.

One of the most important advantages of SaaS companies from a business standpoint is that it's relatively easy to sell them to another company. Consequently, when growing a SaaS company, you're not only making money when it makes a profit; you will also have a handsome payday when you decide to sell it.

Self-Publishing

Thanks to the ebook revolution, it's easier than ever to release your own book. The most successful authors make millions per year publishing their own books, while the less successful ones still make enough to make a comfortable living.

There are two main niches in self-publishing – writing non-fiction books and writing fiction books.

If you consider yourself an expert in a specific area (say gardening), writing non-fiction books is a better choice. You can then grow your company beyond ebooks by releasing online courses, developing membership sites or even offering coaching (if you're up for it).

If you love reading and writing stories, consider writing fiction. You don't even have to write a novel. Many people are looking for short stories to satisfy their craving for entertainment. These titles are usually sold for a much lower price, but they make up for it in volume.

The key to success in self-publishing is to follow the trends. While you can definitely strike it big with a unique idea, you have much higher chances of success if you follow what's already working and give it your own spin.

Self-publishing is one of the most introvert-friendly businesses because your interaction with clients is reduced to a minimum. Except for a few emails from your readers here and there, nobody will bother you.

Blogging

Blogging is perfect for anyone who loves writing and has experience about a specific topic. If you've spent many years living abroad, you can write a blog with tips on how to adapt to a foreign culture. If you're knowledgeable about gardening, you can run a blog for gardeners. If you have experience about survival, you can become known for your blog with tips on how to survive in the wilderness.

Remember that you can only succeed with blogging if you write about a specific how-to topic. Personal blogs about everything and nothing won't cut it if you want to turn them into a business.

Bloggers have a virtually unlimited amount of opportunities to make money on their writing. They can make money releasing ebooks and other digital products, displaying advertising on their sites, recommending products and services of other people, coaching and even selling physical products to their readers.

If you want to become a blogger, consider your blog a platform to build a list of potential customers. The blog in itself is not your main source of revenue. It's just a way to reach your target market and research what it wants to buy.

Keep in mind that the most successful bloggers network a lot with other bloggers. If you can't stand the thought of constantly reaching out to new people and developing online relationships with them, blogging may not be for you.

If networking mostly by email is not a big problem for you, then blogging might be just what you're looking for if you want to make money on your writing and expertise.

Online Courses

Online courses can be either a part of your blogging, podcasting or self-publishing strategy, or they can be your main product. You can either sell your courses on platforms developed for online courses such as Udemy or sell them through your own site and drive paid traffic using Google Adwords or Facebook Ads.

High-end online courses for professionals can be extremely lucrative – if you possess enough experience to create them and make them valuable enough to sell access to them for over $100.

Digital courses are much more introvert-friendly than coaching. For one, you don't have to interact with your clients personally. At most, they will send you an email or two. If you offer coaching, you usually conduct it through Skype, which can drain you of social energy if done for too long or with too many people.

E-Commerce

All types of stores that sell products online are suitable for introverts – as long as they sell small products that don't require a huge warehouse and a team of employees to ship them.

Small e-commerce stores can be managed by one or two people. If you sell products with a high margin (you sell fewer items for a high price), you can usually manage everything on your own without hiring anybody. When shipping and handling becomes too much of a burden, you can either consider hiring an employee to handle it for you or outsource it.

Outsourcing is a good choice if you want to stay location-independent and avoid the headaches of hiring an employee. You can consider selling through a marketplace such as Amazon and benefit from their Fulfillment by Amazon program.

Podcasting

Podcasting is yet another way to build authority as an expert and leverage it to sell digital products and/or coaching. It's similar to blogging, but instead of writing the words, you speak them.

Keep in mind that most successful podcasters usually network a lot and interview a new guest for each episode. Then again, it's another business you can run in your home office without having to meet with anyone in the real world. Everything can be conducted online through Skype.

Mobile apps

Developing mobile apps is yet another idea for introverts with technical minds. If you're capable of coding, developing mobile apps can be a great source of revenue – provided you can come up with apps people need and find interesting enough to share with others.

As in the case of self-publishing, don't count on a huge hit that will take you to seven figures per year. Most developers make money from the sheer quantity of their apps, not from just one or two successful apps.

Newsletter

Running a newsletter is pretty similar to blogging with a small exception – you have much less to worry about. Instead of running a full-blown site, you only have to write regular emails to your subscribers.

Owners of newsletters usually make money through releasing their own digital products, recommending the products of other people (which, while less profitable, has many other benefits) or through selling subscriptions to their newsletter.

The recurring nature of paid newsletters makes them a powerful source of revenue – if you can keep your subscribers paying, of course.

Service-Based Businesses

If you're talented and prefer to run a small one-man operation dependent on your skills, consider freelancing. Some of the most common ways freelancers make money include:

1. Freelance writing. You can either make money writing simple articles for marketers or write more ambitious articles for bigger sites.

2. Copywriting. Professional copywriters can make a fortune writing ads for large, corporate clients.

3. Web design. No online business can exist without a website. You can either focus on local clients or look for gigs on freelancing sites.

4. Graphic design. Choose a specialty (say book cover design) and make yourself an expert in this niche.

5. Editing. People will always write new books and they will always need professional editors to make them easier to read.

6. Translation. If you speak a major foreign language (say, Chinese), you can make a lot of money translating content for corporate clients.

7. Programming. If you don't want to use your programming skills to develop your own software, you can offer them to your clients (sometimes for a small percentage of revenue).

Chapter 7: Choosing the Right Business for You

Choosing the right business for you isn't merely about finding out if it's introvert-friendly. Of course, the key aspects of your business should be as aligned with your preferences as possible, but there are also other aspects to consider.

In this chapter, we'll discuss some of the concepts that are rarely considered by entrepreneurs wishing to start their first business. If you want to succeed, consider these issues before you take action.

Don't Merely Do What You Love

Introverts tend to go deep with everything they find interesting. If they start talking about, say, the afterlife, they can talk about it for hours on end. The same applies to their hobbies – many introverts can't be merely satisfied with being average. They need to become the best.

This behavior can also be seen in business, and it can work to your detriment. If you want to start a business by doing what you love, you may enter the business for the wrong reasons.

Each business starts with finding a need you can fulfill or a problem you can solve. If you have a passion for, say, coffee, you may find it hard to start a successful business as the competition among coffee shops is extremely strong. Besides, the fact that you love coffee doesn't necessarily mean you'll enjoy running a coffee shop.

The right approach to start a business is to make a list of all your strengths and passions, and then see which strength combined with what passion can result in a business people need.

The most important question to ask yourself is always: what need does my business fulfill or what problem does it solve? If you can't come up with a specific answer, your business is probably not such a good idea.

Run a Business that Fits Your Personality

Money and your business' success are obviously important, but if you ever find yourself feeling constantly burned out, consider going into a different business.

I'm a good example of an introvert who got burned out because he chose the wrong business for himself.

I started a software company offering services to businesses. The nature of the business and the fact that most clients weren't as tech-savvy as young people meant that it required numerous phone calls, and for the best results, face-to-face interactions (I didn't even try them, that would completely crush me).

Each day I had to wake up and make 20 or 30 calls. It was a nightmare. Even writing about it now still elevates my heart rate. After a few months of trying to get this business to work for me, I decided to call it quits. And I've been happy ever since, because I found another business that played off my strengths much better. Now that I found the right business for myself, I have never felt more satisfied.

If you constantly feel burned out because of your business, I urge you to ask yourself how long you can keep it this way. Running a business that isn't fit for your personality can cause high levels of stress, anxiety attacks, and even depression. I know it from my experience, because I experienced two of these symptoms myself (and if I kept going, I would have probably experienced severe depression as well).

Money Is Not Everything

A lot of people thinking of starting a business only concern themselves about the money they're going to make if it succeeds. What they forget is that running a business can be an extremely time-consuming endeavor that can negatively affect your personal life.

What are you willing to sacrifice to make your business a success? Do you feel okay with the thought that you'll have less time to spend alone or with your friends? Does the vision of having your mind constantly "on" (if you're an entrepreneur, you never really have time off) scare you?

Entrepreneurship is the best route to riches, but it comes with drawbacks many people tend to overlook. Consider all the side effects of starting and growing a business and ask yourself if you're willing to sacrifice your current lifestyle to develop a better one.

Chapter 8: Introvert-Friendly Ways to Come up with Business Ideas and Test Them

In this chapter, we'll talk how to find business ideas and how to validate them and make sure they can indeed lead to a successful business.

Without proper research, nine times out of ten your business is going to fail. That's why it's extremely important to spend adequate time vouching your idea before you go full time executing it.

How to Come up with Ideas in an Introvert-Friendly Way

The best way to come up with business ideas plays off your strengths as an introvert. Your ability to listen attentively will help you hear numerous business ideas, many of them viable enough to consider testing them.

Whenever you're talking with someone, pay attention to phrases such as, "I hate it when…," "I wish there was…," and, "I need…." Also, listen to complaints, especially when people complain about a bad experience when buying something.

Every time someone says something like this in your presence, see if you can uncover a potential profitable business idea. You don't even have to talk much – just keep asking questions related to the problem for as long as you need to understand it well. If someone admits she would pay to have this problem solved, you pretty much validated the need for this business idea. But don't trust the words alone – ask for the money and gauge the reaction.

Another introvert-friendly way to come up with business ideas is to use various online tools to find potential markets with specific problems to solve or needs to fulfill. Below are a few ways to use the Internet to brainstorm business ideas.

1. Twitter

Twitter is a wonderful place to find frequent complaints and uncover potential gaps in the market.

Use Twitter's search function to find tweets that contain the phrases I mentioned above – "I hate it when," "I wish there was," and so on. You can also look for complaints about specific companies in the industry that interest you to see what they don't do well and find out if you can do it better.

Virtually every social media site can help you discover what other companies do wrong and what they do right. You can also learn what people would like to have and what complaints they have about certain issues in their lives.

2. Discussion boards

Another place where you can look for business ideas are discussion boards about a specific niche, say gardening discussion boards or forums about fashion. As an introvert, you probably like these places a lot because you can interact with people without feeling socially drained. Use Google to find forums about things that interest you and see if anybody has mentioned something that can spark a viable business idea.

You can also create your own thread asking other members about their biggest challenges or problems related to their hobby. Sometimes one simple question can lead you to uncovering a huge gap in the market.

3. Sites for freelancers

If you want to come up with a business service you can perform online while working at your home office, check sites for freelancers such as Odesk or Elance and see what types of jobs are popular. If, for example, you're a great designer, check which design jobs are frequently posted.

An additional benefit of this approach is that you can apply to these jobs to validate if your business idea makes sense. If you want to be a solopreneur, starting with freelancing sites and getting your clients there can be the beginning of a solid small business.

Keep in mind that a service-based business dependent on your skills will never become a proper company that doesn't need you to keep growing – unless you hire other people to replace you.

4. Blogs

As an introvert, you probably read a lot of content online, including blogs. You can check out blogs about things that interest you or things that you do well and see if the bloggers or people commenting on their articles mention any problems they have.

This approach can be extremely effective if you have developed relationships with well-known bloggers – if you solve a problem they have, they may share your product with their readers, thus generating a client base for you.

If you have your own blog, your job is even easier. All you need to do is to ask your readers about their problems and/or products they'd like to have, but don't exist. If you already possess a potential client base, your idea can take off extremely quickly.

5. Google Keyword Planner

Google Keyword Planner, available at https://adwords.google.com/KeywordPlanner, can help you estimate how many people search monthly for a given keyword, say "decorative vases for sale." While it won't tell you how many of these people buy products they find when typing such a keyword, it can tell you if there's any interest at all.

Obviously, not all products are being searched for in Google (especially if it's an innovative product), but it can still help you if you're looking to see how many visitors your online store or blog can get.

Keyword research is a fundamental part of researching ideas for product-based businesses. You should never start selling a product unless you know the estimated number of people who might be interested in buying it.

How to Validate Your Idea in an Introvert-Friendly Way

Thanks to the Internet, it's incredibly easy to validate your business ideas in just a few days to see if you can get any potential clients.

Back in the day, if you wanted to make sure your business could work before starting it, you either had to visit dozens of people or cold call them and ask them if they would be interested in your products or services. Today, you can do the same work in just a few minutes with little to no social interaction.

One way to validate your idea I already mentioned a while ago is to use freelancing sites to see if you can get some clients this way. It's probably the fastest way to enter a service-based business – just create your profile, make it look professional, and start applying for various jobs. Once you get a few clients, word of mouth should help you grow your company.

When applying for jobs at freelance sites, make sure to stand out. You can easily do it by recording a personalized video application. It's something that most freelancers never do, so it's a super easy way to differentiate and show the client how much you care.

If you don't want to start a service-based business, $100-200 is enough to test if your idea to sell products online can gain any traction. What you do is create a simple site describing the basics of your product and drive paid traffic to this site to see if anyone buys it. www.quickmvp.com is a nice tool to help you create such a site and run traffic.

The key is to keep it simple and get the sales page in front of your most likely customers. If after spending $100-200 or so you couldn't get any customers (and all of them were highly targeted), chances are it isn't a good business idea.

The most important aspect of testing your ideas is to test small. If you want to start selling a certain product, order the smallest possible batch and see how it sells. If you need to use paid advertising to find out if your idea has legs, try to gather as much data as possible while spending as little money as possible. In the beginning, each dollar counts – especially if you want to test several ideas.

More detailed advice on how to validate your ideas is beyond the scope of this book. I highly recommend learning about the principles of the lean approach in business to figure out how to test your ideas quickly.

Chapter 9: Productivity for Introverted Entrepreneurs

Introverted entrepreneurs may struggle with time management because they tend to be more overwhelmed by too many tasks in their calendars than extroverts. Extroverts get their high from a lot of things happening at the same time, while introverts need to focus on one thing.

For this reason, introverts should approach their productivity in a slightly different way than extroverts. In this chapter, we'll discuss the three most important aspects of how to be a productive introverted entrepreneur.

Focus on What You're Best At

Introverts need balance in their life much more than extroverts do. Consequently, they prefer to have fewer, but closer friends. They also prefer to have fewer tasks, but work on them for much longer than other people. They prefer to drill one deep hole instead of drilling dozens of shallow holes.

Consequently, the key to high productivity as an introvert is putting focus on what you're best at. Note the keyword here – "best," not merely "good." All of us have exactly twenty-four hours in a day. The more of these hours you spend making yourself stronger in the areas you're already strong, the more effective you'll become.

To give you an example, the best authors focus on only two things: writing and reading. They don't spend much time marketing, designing covers for their books or editing them. They delegate all these things to people who are good at these tasks. As a result, bestselling authors keep sharpening their writing skills instead of wasting time on tasks that aren't necessary to them.

As tempting as it is to try to do everything on your own, don't try to go it alone. Find people who are better than you and use their help. It doesn't necessarily mean you have to hire employees. You can get professional help from many people and pay them by hours worked or a fixed fee.

Protect Your Alone Time

Your alone time is your treasure. If it wasn't for the time spent alone, you would quickly burn out and become much less effective at what you do (if you would be capable of producing anything, for that matter).

Make alone time a part of your daily schedule. Whether you accomplish it through brief meditation sessions interspersed throughout the day, quick walks, reading a book or playing with your pet, it doesn't matter. The key is to take regular breaks at least once per hour (and for the best results, even more often).

I'm a huge believer of the Pomodoro approach where you work for 25 minutes and take a 5 minute break. After four pomodoros (100 minutes of working) you take a longer 15-30 minute break. It's a perfect schedule for everyone who wants to maintain a high level of concentration throughout her entire day. If you work with other people, spend the breaks between each pomodoro in solitude to get even better results.

Don't Waste Time on Meetings and Phone Calls

Most meetings and phone calls are useless. You can get the job done much more quickly by sending a brief email than by taking everyone in your team away from their tasks and making them sit down in a room together.

Avoid unscheduled phone calls at all costs. Most people tend to ramble for a few minutes before they get down to business. If you add up all these minutes, you'll realize you're wasting a couple hours per week listening to useless "let's catch up" drivel.

I have a simple policy. If someone asks me to schedule a call, I ask her if she can condense what she wants to talk about to a few key questions. Then I can answer these questions in just a few minutes, and usually there's no longer need for a call that always takes more time than scheduled.

For the best results while working, never leave your Skype on and silence your phone. One phone call can completely mess up your focus and distract you for much more than the few minutes it takes to end it.

Chapter 10: Most Common Challenges

Introverted entrepreneurs face unique challenges extroverts may not understand. In the following chapter, we'll discuss some of the most common troubles you may experience on your entrepreneurial journey as an introvert.

I Say "Yes" Too Often

Research conducted by Elaine N. Aron and Arthur Aron from the State University of New York at Stony Brook[v] shows that many introverts are highly sensitive people (you can test yourself here to see if you're a highly sensitive person: http://www.hsperson.com/test/highly-sensitive-test/). They process information in a deeper and more reflective way, and thus they do it more slowly.

Unfortunately, many people in business want you to make a decision on the spot. Don't let them modify your decision-making process.

Every time someone pressures you to make a quick decision, don't reply right away. Say, "Let me think about it," and give yourself a second to ponder it. Then you'll avoid saying your default "yes" response right away.

It's especially important when talking over the phone that puts a lot of pressure to reply quickly. Never make a decision on the call – unless you want to regret it.

I Hate Phone Calls

If phone calls make you anxious, don't go into a business that requires you to make them. Trust me. I was in such a business once, and I will never repeat this mistake.

Don't believe that it will get easier if you start making money. If something doesn't fit your personality, it will make you miserable regardless of the money it's making you.

An introverted entrepreneur Dharmesh Shah wrote a great article (http://www.sorrynocalls.com) on why he doesn't take phone calls. You can refer all the people who want to set up a call with you to this article.

I Suck at Negotiating/Direct Selling/Customer Service

Don't go it alone. Nobody is good at everything, and if you suck at some of the aspects of your business because of your personality, don't force yourself to do these things.

It's much better to hire someone to handle these things for you than to try to fit a square peg in a round hole and do these things against your nature.

It's especially important for the key aspects of running your business, such as direct selling and negotiations.

I Want to Run a Perfect Business (Over-Researching)

Introverts love to be prepared. If they could, they would research themselves to death instead of taking action. Let go of this belief and focus on getting practical experience. It can't be gained by reading books; therefore it's much more valuable and insightful.

If you're starting out and don't know which business you should run, pick the first idea you like and do a small test run. If you can get some sales and it doesn't collide with your personality, keep going.

I Feel Burned Out

Introverts risk burnout when they try to do too many things at once with no regard to their personality. If you go without solitude for a long period of time, you're bound to deplete your energy and burn out.

If it happened, there's no other solution but to take a break and recharge your batteries. No matter how difficult it is, find a way to get out for at least a couple days and spend time away from everyone. Whether you spend it at home with a book in your hand or in the wilderness, hiking the mountains, it's up to you. Just get away instead of trying to fight your burnout by burying yourself in work even more.

Learn to avoid burnout in the future by discovering your limitations and respecting your boundaries. If you find it hard to spend hours on long negotiations, don't attend them. Assign an employee to do it for you. If you can't stomach the idea of making a cold call, hire an experienced salesperson for you (or better yet, find a better way to market your services).

All introverts should make it their regular habit to take a few days off and spend them away from everybody. Solitude works like the best medicine for you, so make sure to include alone time in your daily schedule.

Chapter 11: Resource List for Entrepreneurs

Below I list some of my favorite resources for entrepreneurs. Note that I did NOT place any affiliate links here – I receive no compensation whatsoever by recommending these tools to you.

Note: both books and tools are listed in random order.

Books

The Lean Startup: How Today's Entrepreneurs Use Continuous Innovation to Create Radically Successful Businesses by Eric Ries – Understand the principles of the lean philosophy and learn how to manage a startup the right way. It's a must-read for every introverted entrepreneur wishing to run a software-based business. If you're unsure if you want to start one, read this book, too. If it scares you away from starting a software business, consider the investment in it money well spent.

The 4-Hour Workweek: Escape 9-5, Live Anywhere, and Join the New Rich (Expanded and Updated) by Tim Ferriss – One of the best books about creating a lifestyle business (a business structured around your life). If you have no intention of running a huge business and instead want to run a small business that will allow you to lead a comfortable lifestyle, this book is for you.

The $100 Startup: Reinvent the Way You Make a Living, Do What You Love, and Create a New Future by Chris Guillebeau – If you think it takes money to start a business, get this book. It features numerous examples of how to start a company on a shoestring.

The Millionaire Fastlane: Crack the Code to Wealth and Live Rich for a Lifetime by MJ DeMarco – One of the most important books for everyone who wants to start and grow a successful business. If you're new to entrepreneurship, consider it the most important thing you can ever read.

Getting Everything You Can Out of All You've Got: 21 Ways You Can Out-Think, Out-Perform, and Out-Earn the Competition by Jay Abraham – Jay

Abraham is one of the most ingenious business consultants. If you already run a company and want to increase its revenue or reduce its costs, get this book. I highly recommend reading all his books.

The 80/20 Principle: The Secret to Achieving More with Less by Richard Koch – If you want to grow your business more quickly than the competition, you have to focus on the most essential things. This book will teach you how. Koch's approach is introvert-friendly, because it puts focus on doing as little as possible while focusing on just the results.

The ONE Thing: The Surprisingly Simple Truth Behind Extraordinary Results by Gary Keller – It's a perfect book for every introvert who wants to learn how to manage her focus to get the best results. If you want to achieve more by doing less (and which introvert doesn't?), you should get this book now.

Write. Publish. Repeat. (The No-Luck-Required Guide to Self-Publishing Success) by Sean Platt, Johnny B. Truant and David Wright – A must-read for everyone interested in self-publishing. If you want to publish a non-fiction book or a fiction book (whether it's a novel or a shorter work), you need to read this book first.

Nonviolent Communication: A Language of Life by Marshall B. Rosenberg – If you're interested in how to use language to avoid conflicts and understand other people better, grab this book. It depicts a simple process to learn how to empathize with others.

To Sell Is Human: The Surprising Truth About Moving Others by Daniel H. Pink – If you have no idea how to sell, this book will teach you the most effective (and introvert-friendly) way of selling. Jay Abraham (mentioned above) calls it the consultative style of selling. Introverts are even better at it than extroverts.

The E-Myth Revisited by Michael E. Gerber – If you created a business that feels like prison to you, this book will help you create a system that will free you. If you haven't started a business yet, read this book to prevent launching a business that's bound to fall because it was designed the wrong way.

Tools

QuickMVP.com – Useful software to test your ideas. You can set up a quick landing page, run some traffic using Google AdWords and see how many people are interested in your idea.

Adwords.google.com/keywordplanner – Check how many people are searching for specific terms to find out if there's a niche for your product. Keep in mind that the numbers displayed in this tool are just estimates.

Adwords.google.com – If you want to reach highly targeted customers, learn how to advertise your business on Google AdWords. There's a steep learning curve with this network. Don't run ads before you read a book or two on how to do it.

Facebook.com/advertising – If your product has the potential to become viral or appeals to a large market, Facebook Ads may be the best place to advertise your business. As with Google AdWords, it's wise to read a book or two before you start your first campaign.

Fiverr.com – If you want to be a solopreneur, offering your services on Fiverr may be a good idea. The key is to offer more expensive up-sells to your main $5 service. As soon as you grow a customer base, consider taking your business off Fiverr to increase your control.

oDesk.com – oDesk is a great place to look for clients for your professional services. You can also use it to look for remote workers.

Elance.com – Another site for freelancers similar to oDesk. It attracts more professionals than oDesk, so if you don't want to compete with cheap Asian workers, Elance is a better choice.

Shopify.com – Provides one of the easiest ways to set up your e-commerce store. The right e-commerce script will help you increase your conversion rate and make more money per each visitor.

WordPress.org – The best software to run a blog or a website. No matter what kind of a website you want to run, WordPress is usually the best choice.

AWeber.com and Mailchimp.com – two of the best email marketing tools. If you want to have a newsletter, AWeber, MailChimp or a similar service is a must.

Balsamiq.com – An easy way to create a mock-up of your product. Extremely useful to anyone wishing to start a SaaS company.

KDP.amazon.com and Createspace.com – use Amazon to publish your ebooks and use Createspace to publish them as paperbacks.

Udemy.com – an extremely popular platform for digital courses. If you want to make money teaching other people various skills, Udemy can make it easy for you to reach them.

Afterword

As an introvert, you may find entrepreneurship the best career choice for you. It gives you the freedom to socialize with people on your terms instead of being forced to spend 8 hours every single day in a cubicle surrounded by other people.

Entrepreneurship, even if you're just running a small business, is one of the most rewarding things in life. It can give you tremendous satisfaction while providing solutions or fulfilling the needs of other people.

Introversion is a wonderful asset if you want to enter the world of entrepreneurship. I hope my book helped you discover how you, too, can run a business that fits your introverted personality.

Now, do what every entrepreneur at heart values the most: take action and make your dreams come true.

Good luck,

Nate

P.S. Before I write the last words in this book, I'd like to encourage you to sign up for my newsletter for entrepreneurs here: http://eepurl.com/bbVcYX.

As a thank-you gift, you'll get a completely free ebook I used to sell for $2.99 – *15 Steps to Better Time Management and Higher Effectiveness*. You'll also get an opportunity to receive advance reader copies of my new books.

Subscribe to My Newsletter

Sign up for my entrepreneurship newsletter at http://eepurl.com/bbVcYX to receive a completely free ebook I used to sell for $2.99 – *15 Steps to Better Time Management and Higher Effectiveness*. It will teach you how to become a more effective entrepreneur who achieves more with less.

You'll also get exclusive updates about my new titles. Subscribers of my newsletter who are willing to write reviews have the opportunity to get free advance reader copies of my new books.

Don't worry – I don't send emails more often than once per week (and usually less often than that).

Support the Author

Reviews help authors reach more readers. For self-published authors (like me), they're the lifeblood of the business. Your review – even if it's just a quick sentence or two, means the world to me.

I'd love to read your review of my book wherever you bought it.

Books by Nate Nicholson

I write books for people who want to grow and learn new things every single day. Some of the topics I cover in my books include: introversion, happiness, entrepreneurship, and personal growth.

You can access all of my books here: http://www.amazon.com/author/natenicholson.

References

[i] http://www.economist.com/news/science-and-technology/21587195-thinking-about-it-makes-you-better-person-not-worse-one-time-not-money

[ii] http://www.knowyourtype.com/myers-briggs/8_preferences-html/introversion-preference/

[iii] *Business Stripped Bare*, Richard Branson.

[iv] *Screw Business as Usual*, Richard Branson.

[v] http://hsperson.com/pdf/JPSP_Aron_and_Aron_97_Sensitivity_vs_I_and_N.pdf